Jane Goodall

By Catherine Goodridge

Table of Contents

Who Is Jane Goodall? 2

What Did Jane Discover at Gombe? 12

What Work Does Jane Do Now? 18

Who Is Jane Goodall?

Imagine a young woman living in the forests of Africa. Her camp is set up near the shore of a lake. For some months of the year, it rains day and night. Other months are dry and hot. Her neighbors are **chimpanzees**. Every day she watches them and takes notes on what they do. She wants to know what they eat, where they sleep, and how they treat one another.

▲ Chimps spend most of their day feeding and resting.

Soon she is part of the lives of the chimps. She listens to them call to one another across the valleys. She watches them gather in the trees to eat. The chimps learn to trust her. She is able to get close enough to touch them and join in their activities. This is the life that Jane Goodall lived for 15 years.

▲ Jane Goodall, an adventurous woman, greets a "visitor" to her camp in Africa.

Jane Goodall lived in Gombe Stream **National Park** in Africa. There she studied and learned about chimpanzees. She came to know what is special and different about them. The things she discovered during those years changed the way people think of chimpanzees.

Did You Know?

Gombe Stream National Park is a land of forests, valleys, open areas, mountains, and peaks. It is located in Tanzania in Africa. The chimps that live there share their home with bush pigs, baboons, buffalo, leopards, lizards, snakes, birds, and crocodiles.

Jane Goodall was born in London, England, on April 3, 1934. From an early age, she loved animals of all kinds. Her favorite toy was a lifelike chimpanzee. She named it Jubilee in honor of a chimpanzee that had been born in the London Zoo.

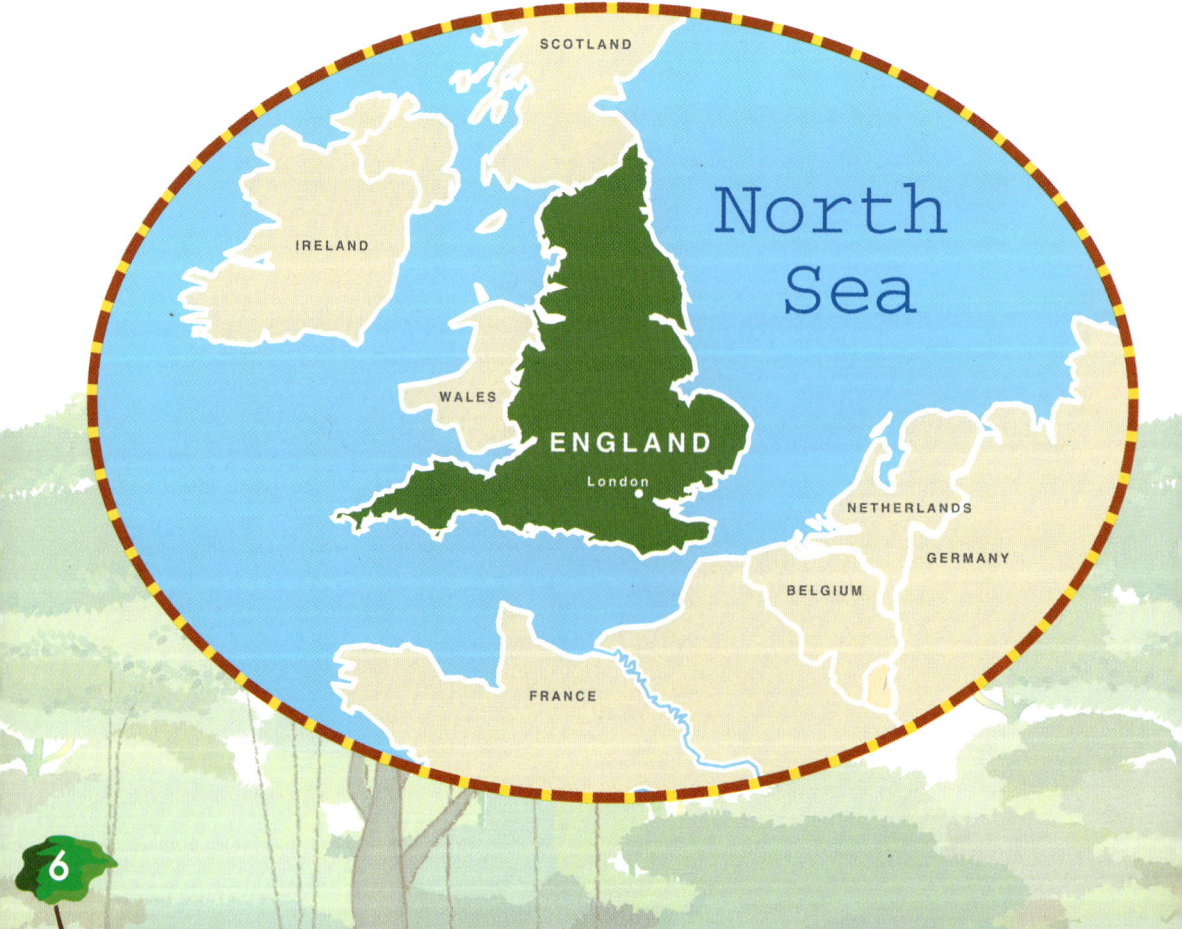

Jane was interested in finding out as much as she could about animals. Her dream was to go to Africa when she grew up. She wanted to live with animals in their natural homes.

▲ Jane's parents gave her Jubilee when she was a baby. She still has him.

In 1957, when she was 23 years old, Jane got the chance to go to Africa. A friend invited her for a visit. Jane saved the money for the trip and left by herself on a ship. She was on her way. Jane's visit to her friend lasted three weeks. When it was over, Jane did not want to leave Africa. She found a job helping a scientist named Louis Leakey. Jane could stay in Africa.

Did You Know?

Louis Leakey (1903–1972) was a scientist who studied the past. He examined ancient bones and fossils, the remains of creatures that lived millions of years ago. He also had an interest in the behavior of chimps.

▲ In this photograph Jane talks with Louis Leakey. It was Leakey who made it possible for Jane to study chimps in the wild.

After three months, Leakey came to Jane with exciting news. There was a group of chimpanzees living in an area far from people. The place was Gombe Stream National Park. Leakey wanted to learn more about these chimps. He knew that learning about the chimps could help scientists understand humans better.

▲ The rolling hills and valleys of Gombe Stream National Park make the park the perfect home for wandering groups of chimps.

Leakey had a plan. He wanted Jane to live at the park. She would observe the chimps in their natural home and write about everything she saw.

Did You Know?

chimp

orangutan

gorilla

Chimpanzees are **primates**, a group of animals that includes apes, monkeys, and humans. Chimpanzees, along with gorillas and orangutans, are apes. Chimps have black, hairy bodies. They have pinkish bare skin on their faces, ears, the palms of their hands, and the bottoms of their feet.

What Did Jane Discover at Gombe?

In 1960, Jane went to Gombe and set up camp by the side of a lake. On the first morning, she went out with her notebook to make contact with the chimps. She saw many chimps, but she could not get close to them. They were afraid of her and fled as soon as they saw her. She followed them carefully through the forest and up the mountainsides. She was scratched, bruised, and tired at the end of the day.

◀ Jane filled notebooks with her observations as she made her first contact with the chimps.

Many weeks later, Jane discovered a high point in the land. She called it the Peak. From this place she could observe the chimps, and they could see that she would not harm them. She watched and recorded what she saw. She made many surprising discoveries.

▲ The chimps find most of their food in trees.

Jane learned that the chimps lived together in **communities**. They moved from place to place, feeding and resting in trees. Most of the time, they were peaceful and friendly. They often greeted one another with hugs and kisses. Sometimes they held hands. Baby chimps played games together on the forest floor. They slept in their mother's arms.

▲ Mother chimps and their babies stay together until the babies are at least 7 years old.

After about a year, Jane was able to get close enough to touch the chimps. Soon, chimps would come to her looking for the bananas that she carried. Then one day, a large chimp came by just to sit with her for a few moments. Jane knew that she had been accepted by the chimps.

▲ Jane soon came to know many of the chimps, and they learned to trust her.

There were about 100 chimps in Gombe. Jane got to know about 50 of them very well. She knew what they were like and what made them different from one another. She discovered that they felt joy and fear and even great sadness. She sometimes used what she knew about a chimp to give it a name.

Did You Know?

Jane chose names for the chimps based on their personality or appearance. One, Mr. McGregor, was bald and reminded Jane of the character Mr. McGregor in the Peter Rabbit books. Another was called David Greybeard because of the color of its long beard. She kept track of families by giving members names with the same first letter. One chimp was named Flo, and her two children were Fifi and Flint. Two brothers were Wilkie and Wulfie. Frodo, Freud, Faust, and Fanny were another group.

Jane discovered that chimps and humans had many things in common. Like humans, chimps use simple tools such as sticks. They communicate with noises and movements. They hunt and share the food they find. They greet one another by touching hands.

Jane loved every part of her life at Gombe. Her discoveries were talked about all over the world.

▲ Chimps are very social and spend most of their time in small groups.

What Work Does Jane Do Now?

Jane left Gombe in 1975, but she has not forgotten the chimps. Today Jane works to improve the lives of chimps in zoos all over the world.

▲ Although many zoos have made life pleasant for their chimps, others keep them in small, crowded cages.

Jane sometimes appears in schools or on television to promote the welfare of chimps and other animals in the wild. When she is not traveling, Jane lives in England. On a chair in her home sits an old stuffed animal named Jubilee.

? Did You Know?

Jane sponsors a program that encourages young people to take a role in protecting the environment. The program is called Roots and Shoots. You can find out more about it by visiting the Jane Goodall Web site: www.janegoodall.org.

▲ Jane travels 300 days a year making speeches and appearances on behalf of animals and the environment.

GLOSSARY

chimpanzees (chim-pan-ZEEZ): African apes; members of the primate family

community (ka-MYOO-nih-tee): a group of people or animals living in the same area

National Park (NASH-uh-nul PARK): land set aside by the government to protect animals that live there

primate (PRYE-mate): a group of animals that includes human beings, monkeys, and apes

INDEX

Gombe Stream National Park	4–5, 10
Leakey, Louis	8–11
primates	11
Roots and Shoots	19